BOOK ANALYSIS

Written by Raphaëlle O'Brien
and Bachir Bourras
Translated by Rebecca Neal

The Yellow Dog

BY GEORGES SIMENON

BOOK ANALYSIS

Bright
≡Summaries.com

Fifty Shades
of Grey Trilogy
BY E. L. JAMES

Shed new light
on your favorite books with

Bright
≡Summaries.com

www.brightsummaries.com

GEORGES SIMENON

BELGIAN WRITER

- **Born in Liège (Belgium) in 1903.**
- **Died in Lausanne (Switzerland) in 1989.**
- **Notable works:**
  - *The Strange Case of Peter the Lett* (1931), novel
  - *The Yellow Dog* (1931), novel
  - *Pedigree* (1948), novel

The prolific Belgian writer Georges Simenon began his career as a journalist before going on to write over 190 novels and numerous short stories, which were published either under his own name or under a pseudonym.

When he was starting out as a writer, the French author Colette (1873-1954) advised him to focus on creating simple stories rather than trying to write great literature. Simenon took her words to heart and used a straightforward, unadorned style to describe the society of his time and depict the lives of ordinary people, as well as the dark underbelly of politics and criminality.

Simenon travelled widely, was insatiably curious and wrote at an incredible rate: he could complete an entire novel by working continuously for 11 days. In 2003, the prestigious *Bibliothèque de la Pléiade* published a two-volume collection of his works, clearly indicating his importance in the world of French-language literature.

THE YELLOW DOG

ONE OF THE EARLIEST MAIGRET NOVELS

- **Genre:** detective novel
- **Reference edition:** Simenon, G. (2006) *The Yellow Dog*. Trans. Asher, L. New York: Penguin.
- **1st edition:** 1931
- **Themes:** investigation, suspense, murder, revenge, fear, smuggling

The Yellow Dog was published in 1931 and is one of the earliest works centring on Superintendent Maigret, who first appeared in a novel published earlier that year. In this novel, the detective is still unmarried, but is already smoking his famous pipe.

He is tasked with solving a string of crimes in the small town of Concarneau in Brittany, where he grows close to some of the humble inhabitants and takes them under his wing. In this novel, Simenon paints an uncompromising picture of the provincial bourgeoisie and develops his character's unconventional investigative techniques.

SUMMARY

A NEW INVESTIGATION BEGINS

The story begins in Concarneau at 11pm on 7 November. After leaving the local Admiral Hotel, Monsieur Mostaguen steps into the doorway of a seemingly empty house to light his cigar, where he is shot by a mystery attacker hiding in the house. Just afterwards, a yellow dog appears out of nowhere and lies down in the hotel café.

Superintendent Maigret and his young companion Inspector Leroy arrive the following day. Maigret meets with Jean Servières, Le Pommeret and Dr Michoux, who spent the evening with Mostaguen. As the three men are about to drink their customary Pernod, Michoux stops them, having noticed that a deposit of white powder has formed at the bottom of their glasses. The powder is analysed and identified as strychnine, a deadly poison. Michoux decides to sleep at the hotel and Maigret questions Emma, the hotel's waitress and Michoux's occasional mistress, who seems deeply shaken by the crime.

The following day, Maigret realises that the yellow dog has disappeared. Someone claims to have seen it in Michoux's garden, but the doctor refuses to go see it. When Maigret goes to the house, he finds both human and dog footprints.

Back at the hotel, he learns that Servières has disappeared. His car is found by the river some time later, with bloodstains on the seat. Maigret notices that the yellow dog has come back and is lying at Emma's feet. Michoux is terrified and shuts himself away in his room. At this stage, Maigret sees him, Servières and Le Pommeret as unremarkable men who are trying to keep up appearances.

The local newspaper, the *Brest Beacon*, publishes an anonymous sensationalist article which claims that a dangerous local vagrant is responsible for the murder.

In the late afternoon in the old town, someone shoots the yellow dog. Maigret arranges for it to be treated, but it disappears again. A swarm of journalists descend on the hotel. Le Pommeret, who had drunk his aperitif there, is found dead at his home, and the autopsy reveals that he died of strychnine poisoning. However, an analysis of the glass he drank from reveals no trace of the poison.

The mayor then demands an arrest, so Maigret issues an arrest warrant for Michoux. The detective has deduced that the doctor is in fact the next intended victim, so he orders the prison guard not to let anybody enter. A vagrant is also arrested by two policemen, but manages to escape. Maigret does not attach any importance to this incident. One of the policemen accompanies him to Cabélou Point, where he finds food remains that indicate that the vagrant has been living there for a week.

At 11pm, Leroy meets Maigret on the roof of the hotel to observe the empty house the vagrant is sleeping in. The vagrant is joined by Emma, and the two of them argue before sharing a passionate embrace and leaving the house.

A customs guard falls victim to another murder attempt. After checking that Michoux is unharmed, Maigret receives a telegram: Servières, whom Leroy had said was in Brest, has just been arrested in Paris. The mayor demands a meeting with Maigret, who shows him that any of the customers in the café at the Admiral Hotel could be behind the murders, then asks him about Michoux. He learns that the doctor and his mother are involved in property dealings as a way of making more money. Before he leaves, Maigret says that the case will be solved the following day.

THE MYSTERY IS SOLVED

Maigret and Leroy search Emma's room, where they find a letter from a man named Léon, who writes that he has bought a boat called the *Pretty Emma* and will soon be able to marry her. The two men then head to the room where Michoux was staying, where Maigret deciphers a message that was written in the room and learns that Emma is planning to meet the vagrant in the deserted house.

Maigret summons the mayor, Madame Michoux, Servières, Emma and the vagrant to the police station. Michoux is very agitated, but Maigret manages to calm him down: "In a few moments, I expect the murderer to be right here within these four walls" (p. 126).

He then questions the people present to find out what happened on board the *Pretty Emma* five or six years previously. According to the mayor, the boat was inspected in New York and cocaine was found on board.

Maigret turns to the vagrant, who is actually the Léon of Emma's letter, and asks him for his version of events. He tells him that at the time, Michoux, Servières, Le Pommeret and an American proposed that he get involved in smuggling. Once he reached the USA, Léon was arrested and incarcerated in the Sing Sing prison in New York, where he met the American by chance. The American told him that the three others, who wanted to get their hands on the monetary reward offered for reporting smuggling, had sold the *Pretty Emma*, and saw to his release.

Now that he was free and his only friend in the world was a yellow dog who was raised on board the boat, Léon swore to make the three other men pay by ensuring that they too experienced the horrors of prison. Léon then sought out Michoux in the hope that he would shoot him and be arrested. Michoux was terrified and wanted to get rid of Léon, so he asked Emma to write a letter asking him to meet her in the empty house. However, Léon did not fall for the trap, so it was Mostaguen who ended up in the wrong place at the wrong time and was shot instead.

When he arrived the next day, Maigret could tell that the three men were expecting something dramatic to happen and observed their reactions very closely. Servières wrote the article in the *Brest Beacon* to cast suspicion on Léon, before staging an attack and faking his own death. When Michoux thought that Le Pommeret was about to reveal the secret, he poisoned him.

When Léon came back to pick up the yellow dog – which is now dead – the police arrested him, but he managed to run away. Maigret had Michoux arrested, both to keep him safe and to prevent him from doing any more harm. His mother tried to dispel any suspicions surrounding him by shooting at the first passerby she saw when he was in prison. Léon stayed nearby as he did not want to let Michoux escape. However, Emma came back to him and convinced him that if they fled they could start a new life together.

Michoux and his mother are then arrested: he is sentenced to 20 years' forced labour and she faces three months in prison. Servières is tried for obstruction of justice, while Emma and Léon, who have now been exonerated, move to Le Havre thanks to the money that Maigret gives them.

CHARACTER STUDY

THE INVESTIGATORS

Maigret

The famous detective Maigret already has a great deal of experience by the time he embarks on this investigation. He is in Concarneau because "[f]or the past month he [has] been assigned to Rennes to reorganize its mobile unit" (p. 6).

Simenon does not describe Maigret in detail: all we know is that he is large and stocky, and constantly smokes his pipe. The most striking thing about him is his behaviour: the narrator says that "it could be unsettling to see his large eyes stare blankly at you [...] then hear him mutter something incomprehensible and move on as if you were not worth noticing" (p. 51).

His impassiveness stands out most when he is with people who are losing control of themselves. While Michoux is seized by terror, Maigret is "like the antithesis of [...] agitation, fever, sickness

[...] of that unwholesome and repellent terror" (p. 75). This imperviousness is also reflected in his investigative methods: unlike Leroy, Maigret says that he never bases his approach on deductions or unprovable beliefs, but rather sticks to the facts. In fact, he tells the awestruck young inspector that "in this case [...] my method has actually been not to have one" (p. 114).

Leroy

Leroy is a young "inspector with whom [Maigret has] not worked before" (p. 6), and has only just graduated from police school. He is 25 years old and "look[s] more like what's called a well-bred young man than a police inspector" (p. 15). In spite of his relative naivety and lack of experience, which Maigret looks on with a kind of ironic indulgence, he is conscientious and driven, and the detective comes to trust him more and more as the story progresses.

THE ORDINARY PEOPLE

Emma

Emma is the waitress at the Admiral Hotel's café. She wears a black skirt, white apron and Breton headdress. She immediately inspires sympathy in Maigret because of "her long face with its sunken eyes and thin lips [and] [h]er Breton lace cap [which] was slipping as usual to the left on her unkempt hair" (p. 13). Although her face has "no particular grace" (p. 8), Maigret finds it "so appealing" (*ibid*.) that he can "hardly [stop] watching it" (*ibid*.).

The narrator paints a somewhat contradictory picture of her: "She was anemic. Her flat chest was not formed to rouse desire. Nevertheless, she had an odd attraction, perhaps because she seemed troubled, discouraged, unhealthy" (pp. 18-19). After they watch her embrace Léon, Maigret and Léon realise that "[s]he [is] beautiful! Everything about her [is] appealing, even her flat figure, her black dress, her red eyelids" (p. 90).

She is quiet and unassuming, and seems to be worn down by her miserable life, in which her occasional flings with Michoux and Le Pommeret bring her no pleasure or hope. She was formerly in love with Léon, but does not know what has become of him. By watching her closely, Maigret discerns that there is "an exaggerated humility about her" (p. 18): "And yet he sensed, beneath that image, glints of pride held firmly in check" (*ibid.*). Indeed, she is the one who attempts to poison the plotters when she realises that Michoux is trying to entrap Léon, and she manages to persuade her lover to change his plans.

Léon Le Gléric

Léon Le Gléric is the vagrant that the police and the prominent citizens of Concarneau are pursuing. His defining feature is his physique: he is far bigger than the average man, and has enormous hands. Maigret affectionately refers to him as "my bear" (p. 76) and "this man with big feet" (p. 35), and we are told that "[h]is head was hunched into his shoulders, and his sweater showed off his chest muscles" (p. 87).

His cropped hair, "two broken teeth, right in the middle [of his mouth]" (p. 68) and hand tattoos ("an anchor, on the left hand, with the letters S S on both", p. 67) hint at his difficult past, which included a stint in Sing Sing prison (hence the letters "S S").

The end of the novel reveals him to be a man with simple dreams (he just wants to marry Emma and live on a boat) who got caught up in the dishonest schemes of Concarneau's notables. He is too simple to hatch a complicated plot for revenge and is planning to give up his life, until Emma makes him see that the life they dreamed of is still possible. However, their happy ending would have been unattainable without Maigret's help.

The yellow dog

The yellow dog "turn[s] up from somewhere" (p. 2) when the first crime is committed. It is described as "a dirty yellow" (p. 4) colour and "tall and lanky, very thin" (*ibid*.). It quickly comes to be seen as a harbinger of or accomplice to the crimes, and the townspeople get so caught up in the excitement surrounding its appearances and disappearances that a shoemaker falls victim to the collective hysteria and shoots it.

After Léon left Concarneau for America, the dog was his only friend: he "raised him onboard, and he'd saved [him] from drowning once. In spite of all their rules over there [at Sing Sing], they let him stay in the prison" (p. 136). The dog dies from its wounds after being shot, and Léon surreptitiously takes it away to bury it in Cabélou.

THE NOTABLES

The mayor

The mayor is "a very well-groomed elderly man with a small white goatee; his gestures [are] curt" (p. 48). He is from an old local family which owns most of the land in the area, and feels an affinity for his fellow notables. His family is wealthy and has good taste, as can be seen from his lifestyle and elegant, opulent villa.

He is an authoritarian figure: he asks Maigret to solve the case, and becomes impatient and even resorts to threats when the detective does not arrest the perpetrator quickly enough for his liking. However, he is a good sport and comes to respect Maigret and his abilities.

Ernest Michoux and his mother

Ernest Michoux and his mother are the novel's principal wrongdoers. The old woman only appears at the end of the story, "in a mauve dress and wearing her jewels, powder and rouge" (p. 127). Her perfume has "a sugary violet scent" (p. 130) that gives people headaches. She is also very cantankerous and tries to use her family connections to intimidate other people (her late husband was a deputy). As the novel closes, she is trying to secure a retrial for her son by pulling strings with her political connections.

Michoux is central to the plot. He is a "doctor on paper only [...] since he's never practiced" (p. 7). After failing to establish a successful career and being left by his wife because of his lack of ambition, he has led a dissolute lifestyle and lived beyond his means. He is sickly (he claims to have kidney problems and to have had one kidney removed) and quite physically repulsive, with "a thin young rooster's neck with a yellowish Adam's apple bulging from it" (p. 146).

Léon's reappearance leaves him paralysed with fear, and he wanders around the Admiral Hotel "white as a sheet, his features drawn, nostrils pinched, lips drained of color" (p. 138). However, his cowardice is partly a ploy to make Maigret think that he is harmless. It is also a façade which conceals his selfishness and determination to protect his own interests at any cost, even if it means resorting to betrayal (Léon) and murder (Le Pommeret).

During his trial, he grows "steadily thinner, yellower, sicklier, but he never [gives] up" (p. 149), and is always coming up with ways to make the proceedings drag on for longer. The last time we see him, as he is leaving for Devil's Island to serve his sentence of forced labour, he is "still skinny and yellow, with his crooked nose, a bag on his back, and a forage cap on his head" (p. 150).

Yves Le Pommeret

Le Pommeret is killed by Michoux so that he cannot reveal the notables' role in Léon's fate. His "manner and voice show him to be a leading citizen" (p. 4). He has "a fine silver mustache, smoothly slicked hair, a fair complexion and florid cheeks" (p. 7), and is described as "an unrepentant skirt-chaser, a man of independent means and vice-consul for Denmark" (*ibid.*).

He has a bad reputation in the area because he uses his status as a noble to seduce young working-class girls. The thing that stands out the most over the course of the investigation is the fact that he lives far beyond his means: his brother describes him as "an absolute good-for-nothing" (p. 79) and says that he has "a mania for running up bills and for playing the lord of the manor" (*ibid.*), which explains why he finds himself so desperately short of money.

Jean Servières

Out of the three conspirators, Jean Servières (not his real name) is the least guilty, even though, like the other two, he is a failure who lives beyond his means and sometimes behaves dissolutely. He is "a plump little man" (p. 5) and works as the editor of the *Brest Beacon*. He claims that he left his native Paris to live out his retirement in Concarneau, but Maigret finds out that he actually got himself into a difficult situation in the capital which forced him to flee. He is so panicked by Léon's reappearance that he pens a sensationalist (and entirely false) article before faking his own death. He is keenly aware of newspapers' power to shape public opinion, and hopes that the town's inhabitants will panic and pursue the vagrant.

ANALYSIS

THE NOVEL'S SOCIOLOGICAL DIMENSION

A realist novel

In his seminal work *Les romanciers du réel. De Balzac à Simenon* ("The Novelists of the Real: From Balzac to Simenon"), the Belgian literary theorist Jacques Dubois (born in 1933) traces the development of realism and argues that, beginning with Guy de Maupassant (French writer, 1850-1893), the movement's writers sought to attain a greater understanding of humanity. He argues that subsequent writers focused less on describing the world objectively than on depicting the way reality is filtered through an individual's consciousness (Dubois, 2000: 59).

This remark applies to Simenon's novels, including *The Yellow Dog*, as the geographical and social reality depicted in the story is constructed from Maigret's perspective. The image of the detective "watching their faces from the corner of his eye" (p. 24) recurs throughout the text. Although we could be forgiven for thinking that his view of reality is somewhat restricted, his surreptitious observation actually allows him to pick up myriad minor details and gain a greater understanding of the situation without giving away his own feelings. For example, when he goes to see the mayor, he is quick to notice everything about the other man's appearance, including "his white hair, his silk-trimmed smoking jacket, his sharply creased gray trousers" (p. 106), while "[i]t would have been impossible to guess Maigret's thoughts" (*ibid.*).

Simenon's extensive use of dialogue allows us to classify the different characters based on how they express themselves. Written correspondence plays a similar role, as can be seen in Emma's letter in Chapter 9, which is filled with misspelt words and grammatical errors.

Given the novel's brief length (it comes in at around 150 pages), no detail is superfluous, and the many descriptive touches all play a role in the narrative.

A social novel

To fully understand *The Yellow Dog* and the rest of Simenon's work, it is essential to take the author's outlook on humanity into consideration. Specifically, he believed that each individual is shaped by two factors: their social background and their past. Although they can change their social status, this transformation is only superficial and cannot fully erase who they were to begin with. This principle is illustrated in *The Yellow Dog* through the character of Michoux.

Simenon was deeply committed to the idea of fully knowing humankind and stripping away the superficial adornments that hide people's true natures. He took an almost scientific approach to this task, and Dubois has described his novels as "laboratories" in which he experiments with his characters. Consequently, some see Simenon as a direct descendent of Émile Zola (French writer, 1840-1902), the leading figure of the naturalist movement, who sought to use his novels to examine the consequences of placing particular characters in specific circumstances and social environments.

In this sense, the crimes in Simenon's novels and the subsequent investigations by Maigret can be seen as a pretext to allow the author to explore various social environments. The town thus becomes a confined, rigid setting that the characters struggle to escape from.

In sociological terms, the descriptions of the characters serve to classify them into types based on their social background and their past. When Emma appears for the first time, we are given a description of her clothing and physical appearance: "her long face with its sunken eyes and thin lips [and] [h]er Breton lace cap [which] was slipping as usual to the left on her unkempt hair" (p. 13). The physical description which follows this can be also interpreted symbolically:

> "There was an exaggerated humility about her. Her cowed eyes, her way of gliding noiselessly and carefully about, of quaking with anxiety at the slightest word, were the very image of a scullery maid accustomed to hardship." (p. 18)

Once we find out about Emma's troubled past and fraught relationships with men, it becomes possible to interpret her slipping cap as a symbol of her difficult life.

Her character seems to consist of three different aspects:

- the person she is, which is immediately visible;
- the person she was, which can be glimpsed in the person she currently is;
- the person she will be, which the author believes is shaped by social determinism and by her past.

The dialogue featured in the novel, and more specifically the proportion of speech allotted to each character, is also revealing with regard to the class struggle between the powerful characters (the mayor, Michoux and Le Pommeret) and their weaker counterparts (Emma and Léon, who is given the dehumanising nickname of the "bear"). Emma and Léon speak very little: Léon only speaks at the end of the novel, and even though Emma is present throughout the narrative, she seems to be relegated to the role of a worried observer and appears incapable of influencing the world around her.

Social hierarchies in a small provincial town

Concarneau is virtually cut off from the rest of the world, and seems to be a somewhat stifling microcosm of society "where everyone knows everyone else" (p. 24) and the inhabitants are constantly observing one another. Even though Maigret is a complete outsider, the day after his arrival "he realize[s] that everyone already [knows] who he [is]" (p. 33).

The most salient feature of this town is the exceptionally strict hierarchy which governs its inhabitants: the ordinary people are treated as insignificant, viewed with contempt and shamelessly manipulated by the notables, whom they dislike and whose decline they take pleasure in, although they do not go so far as to openly oppose them.

When some of the town's leading citizens are murdered, a young police officer explains that the ordinary people do not seem too upset, and are even almost pleased about what is happening. The notables constantly rub their purported superiority in their fellow citizens' faces: "And in the summer it was worse, with their Paris friends. They were always drinking, making a racket in the streets at two in the morning, as if the town belonged to them" (p. 64).

This hierarchy, which allows a small handful of powerful citizens to dominate the majority, for whom they have nothing but contempt, explains why some people are prepared to do anything to maintain their social position, even when their money has run out. The three notables find themselves in this situation but try to conceal or escape their penury through cocaine smuggling, sketchy property dealings (Michoux and his mother), or debts and false appearances (Le Pommeret).

Although it is tempting to see *The Yellow Dog* as a critique of provincial narrow-mindedness, Léon's experience in Sing Sing ("There were rich prisoners who went off into town almost every night... and they used the rest of us as their servants!", p. 134) suggests that this situation is not unique to the small French town where the story is set, but is present in all human societies.

FEAR

After he has solved the crime, Maigret says that fear "underlies this whole business" (p. 143). Indeed, on both and individual and a collective level, fear is the predominant emotion in *The Yellow Dog*.

Perhaps the clearest example of this is Michoux, who shuts himself up in his hotel room and is "a picture of panic at its most pathetic and repellent" (p. 122). However, he is far from the only victim of fear; indeed, the entire population of Concarneau is afraid. It is as though the townspeople are beginning to be seized by a sort of collective psychosis. For example, after Servières fakes his own death, "[i]n less than a quarter of an hour the streets had emptied, and when footsteps sounded, they were the hurried ones of someone anxious to get to the shelter of home" (p. 42).

Michoux's remark that "[i]t's easy enough for strong people to despise cowards. But they ought to take the trouble to learn where the cowardice comes from" (p. 73) is thought-provoking. The doctor is trying to throw Maigret off the scent by portraying himself as a powerless victim, but his comment also serves as a reminder that fear has a cause and that some people can inspire fear at will. Indeed, the powerful men in *The Yellow Dog* use their relationships with others to force people to obey them. For example, the mayor tries to intimidate Maigret into completing his investigation more quickly.

The use of fear is not always so overt and straight-forward. At the end of the novel, Maigret reveals that, while Michoux pretended to be afraid, he and his accomplices were almost able to use fear to eliminate the man who was terrorising them. Based on the principle that a "panicky crowd is capable of anything" (p. 142), Michoux and Servières attempted to sow fear throughout Concarneau so that one of the town's inhabitants would shoot Léon.

Furthermore, Simenon criticises the press's power to do harm by showing how newspapers can manipulate public opinion under the guise of imparting information. In Servières's article for the *Brest Beacon*, "[e]very sentence is calculated to spread terror in Concarneau" (*ibid.*). The column immediately has the desired effect, and the hysteria sweeping through the town mounts even further when a horde of journalists from Paris descends on Concarneau. The journalists want to sell more newspapers and are only too willing to believe that a threat is looming over the town without even a shred of proof. Simenon incorporates sensationalist articles into his novel to show how their writers sacrifice facts and the truth in order to manipulate people's emotions.

A DETECTIVE NOVEL

The genre of detective fiction began to develop during the 18th and 19th centuries, although some critics have traced its origins back to antiquity.

Detective novels differ from thrillers, which aim to inspire fear and are linked to the English Gothic novel, in that they are centred around the resolution of a crime.

The short story *The Murders in the Rue Morgue* (1841) by the American writer Edgar Allan Poe (1809-1849) is widely recognised as the first modern detective story and introduced the rigorous investigative approach that came to characterise the genre. Poe's detective Dupin uses scientific, strictly logical methods, and these traits were emulated by later characters, such as Sherlock Holmes, the most famous creation of the British writer Arthur Conan Doyle (1859-1930).

At first glance, the novels and short stories featuring Superintendent Maigret, beginning with *The Strange Case of Peter the Lett* (1931), do not seem to offer anything new: like in all detective novels, the main character is presented with a crime which they must investigate and solve. However, Maigret's approach to the investigation differs from that of his predecessors, as he is not interested in the crime itself, but in the criminal. This explains why he focuses less on logical rigour than many other fictional detectives. In *The Yellow Dog*, Leroy symbolises the scientific approach, whereas Maigret represents a more intuitive method. He seems to be guided by his whims, which often makes it difficult for the reader to follow what he is doing and frustrates the other characters, who think that his investigation is stalling until he brilliantly reveals the culprit at the end of the story. The fact that he eschews a chronological, strictly rational approach gives Maigret a unique place in the history of detective fiction.

MAIGRET'S METHOD

Maigret's investigative method is not what we have come to expect from a fictional detective and can seem paradoxical:

> "You're lucky, my friend! Especially in this case, in which my method has actually been not to have one. I'll give you some advice: if you're interested in getting ahead, don't take me for a model, or invent any theories from what you see me doing." (p. 114)

In spite of his claims, the detective does have his own method, which can be seen in *The Yellow Dog* and a number of Simenon's other novels. This method can be divided into three distinct stages:

- **The immersion phase**, during which Maigret engages with his surroundings in order to get to know the place and the people living there (Chapters 1 to 7). This is the longest phase. In it, we see Maigret sitting down smoking his pipe, and it is almost as if he is outside time and space. He pays little attention to physical clues, instead using his suspicious, inquisitive mind to identify even the smallest behavioural indicators. Compared with his younger colleague Leroy, who employs traditional investigative methods, Maigret seems to be groping in the dark and moving very slowly, which angers the mayor and may also frustrate the reader. He progresses steadily and often seems to be daydreaming, which contrasts with his ungainly appearance and heavy footsteps to make him a complex, paradoxical character. The difference in the two characters' approaches gives rise to comical situations; for example, when Léon embraces Emma, "Leroy sound[s] overcome" (p. 89), while Maigret "nearly burst[s] out laughing" (*ibid.*).

- **The investigation phase**, which in *The Yellow Dog* spans Chapters 8 and 9. Maigret enters locations which were previously off limits to the reader, namely Emma and Michoux's rooms, and seems to start attaching more importance to physical clues: he picks up a postcard, then a letter signed by Léon. During this phase the detective makes suppositions about the course of the characters' lives which are then confirmed in the third and final phase.

- **The confrontation phase**, in which the

victims, perpetrators and representatives of the forces of justice and order come together (Chapters 10 and 11). The other two phases are dependent on this one, as is hinted when Maigret tells Leroy that he "ran this investigation from the end, backward" (p. 114). At this point, the events of the plot are placed in chronological order and the truth comes out. Léon, the victim who is desperate for revenge, finally gets the chance to speak, and his words are accompanied by those of the detective.

In *The Yellow Dog*, Maigret is clearly far less interested in the intrigue than in the individuals behind it. His human side sometimes leads him to stray from the ethics than normally govern police work; in this case, he shields Emma from the force of the law even through she has attempted to kill multiple people. He therefore remains an atypical, unique detective right to the end.

FURTHER REFLECTION

SOME QUESTIONS TO THINK ABOUT...

- Study the novel's setting, in terms of physical location, environment and atmosphere. In what ways does it help to generate suspense?
- What are the effects of the novel's treatment of time (the duration of the narrative and its chronology)?
- Observe Maigret's method. What does he base his investigation on? What elements does he pay particular attention to, and what elements does he more or less ignore?
- Michoux tells Maigret that "[i]t's easy enough for strong people to despise cowards. But they ought to take the trouble to learn where the cowardice comes from" (p. 73). In the context of *The Yellow Dog*, how do you interpret this remark?
- Examine the role that the media, particularly newspapers, play in the investigation. How could the way the journalists use information about the ongoing investigation be dangerous?

- Do you think that the media still uses fear to manipulate public opinion? Justify your answer.
- Study the scene of the final confrontation and the revelation of the guilty party. What traditional elements of detective fiction feature in this scene?
- In what ways is Simenon critical of the middle classes in *The Yellow Dog*? Do you think he is more sympathetic to the working-class characters? Justify your answer.
- Some critics have highlighted a number of weaknesses in the Inspector Maigret series, particularly with regard to the detective's behaviour. Have you noticed any of these weaknesses?
- Literary critics have often judged Simenon's work harshly, particularly because of its style. Why do you think this is? Do you think their criticism is justified?

We want to hear from you!
Leave a comment on your online library
and share your favourite books on social media!

FURTHER READING

REFERENCE EDITION

- Simenon, G. (2006) *The Yellow Dog*. Trans. Asher, L. New York: Penguin.

REFERENCE STUDIES

- Dubois, J. (2000) *Les romanciers du réel. De Balzac à Simenon*. Paris: Seuil.

ADAPTATIONS

- *The Yellow Dog*. (1932) [Film]. Jean Tarride. Dir. France: Les Établissements Braunberger-Richebé.

- Le Chien Jaune. (1968). *Les enquêtes du commissaire Maigret*. [TV programme]. Antenne2, 24 February 1968.

- Le Chien Jaune. (1988). *Les enquêtes du commissaire Maigret*. [TV programme]. Antenne2, 13 March 1988.

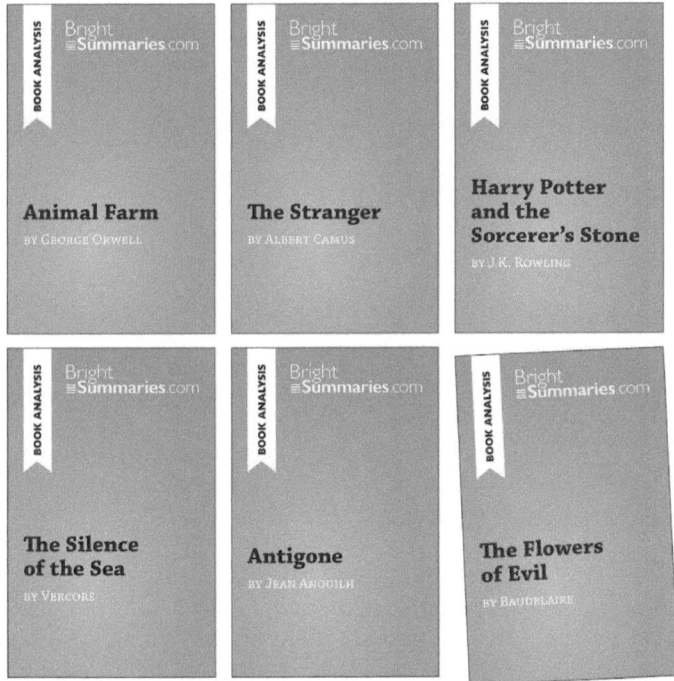

www.brightsummaries.com

Ebook EAN: 9782808010405

Paperback EAN: 9782808010412

Legal Deposit: D/2018/12603/257

This guide was written with the collaboration of
Bachir Bourras for the sections "A realist novel",
"A social novel", "A detective novel" and "Maigret's
method".

Cover: © Primento

Digital conception by Primento, the digital partner
of publishers.